LARS PORSENA

LARS PORSENA

*Or The Future of Swearing
and Improper Language*

ROBERT GRAVES

Martin Brian & O'Keeffe
London

First published in 1927 by
Kegan, Paul, Trench, Trubner & Co Ltd
This edition published in 1972
by Martin Brian & O'Keeffe Ltd
37 Museum Street London WC1

ISBN 0 85616 030 X

Printed in Great Britain
by W & J Mackay Limited, Chatham

FOREWORD

This book, which I wrote while I was Professor of English at Cairo University in 1926, during the General Strike, is now resurrected as an interesting historical curiosity.

Swearing has now virtually ended in Britain, except for words like 'bloody' and 'fucking', still commonly used as intensives. This is because the age of sexual permissiveness initiated by the Pill makes pornography no longer either legally punishable or morally shocking; because the almost total decay of religious faith has taken all the punch out of mere blasphemy.

Mallorca, 1971   ROBERT GRAVES

LARS PORSENA

Of recent years in England there has been a notice-
able decline of swearing and foul language, and
this, except at centres of industrial depression,
shows every sign of continuing until a new shock
to our national nervous system, a European war on
a large scale or widespread revolutionary disturb-
ances at home, may (or may not) revive the habit of
swearing, simultaneously with that of praying.
While, therefore, obscene and blasphemous tongues
are temporarily idle, it would be well to inquire
intelligently into the nature and necessity of their
employment: a ticklish theme and one seldom pub-
licly treated except in comminations from orthodox
pulpits. It is to be hoped that this essay will steer
its difficult course without private offence to the
reader as without public offence to the Censor.

To begin with a few necessary commonplaces.
The chief strength of the oath in Christian countries, and indeed everywhere, is that it is forbidden
by authority, and the Mosaic injunction against
taking the name of Jehovah in vain must mark the

beginning of our research. This commandment seems to have had a double force, recording in the first place a taboo against the mention, except on solemn occasions, of the tribal god's holy name (for so among certain savage tribes it is still considered unlucky to use a man's real name, often only known to himself and the priest), and in the second place a taboo against the misuse of even a decent periphrasis of the god's name: for the act of calling him to witness any feat or condition, or the summons to curse or destroy an enemy, must involve elaborate purifications or penalties. Any vain appeal to God to witness or punish a triviality was therefore forbidden as lessening not only the prestige of religion but also the legal dues of the priestly commissioners of oaths. Now however that the economic interest has dwindled, and priesthood has been shorn of temporal powers, the vain oath is no longer punishable with stoning or with the stake—it is regarded merely as a breach of the peace. 'Goddam you, sir, for your interference,' spoken to a railway company official, is not liable to greater penalties than 'To the pigs with dirty King William', spoken in Belfast. Though the railwayman is given credit for possible religious fanaticism, and though the goddam-er is formally reminded of the solemn nature of the oath when he kisses the Book in the witness-box, the Almighty is left to avenge the spiritual fault personally.

The taboo on vain mention of God or Gods is also extended to the divine mysteries, to the sacraments and sacred writings, and to the human representatives of Heaven where they are permitted direct communion with the Absolute. In Catholic countries, Saints and Prophets are, therefore, used for swearing in a low key, and it has meant a serious lessening of the dignity of the Almighty in England that Protestantism and Dissent have removed these valuable intermediaries from objurgation as from adoration. In Catholic countries, too, the Bible is not vulgarly broadcast, and an oath by the Great Chained Word of God is resonant and effective; while in England the prolific output of sixpennyworths and even pennorths of the Holy Scriptures from secular presses has further weakened the vocabulary of the forceful blasphemer. The triumph of Protestantism is, perhaps, best shown by the decline into vapidity of 'By George!', the proudest oath an Englishman could once swear; for the fact is we have lost all interest in our Patron Saint. It has been stated with detail and persistence that in the late summer of 1918 an Australian mounted unit sensationally rediscovered the actual bones of St George—not George of Cappodocia but the other one who slew the Dragon: they were brought to light by the explosion of a shell in the vault of a ruined church. The officer in command sent a cable to the Dean and Chapter of Westminster inviting them to house the holy relics. After some delay, the Dean and Chapter formally regretted the serious overcrowding of their columns, for, of course, though they could not very well mention it, St George was a bloody German. So the Saint was lost again by the disgusted Australians, this time beyond rescue. Or so one version of the story has it. The other version, more attractive if less authenticated, suggests that the Dean relented later and permitted the relics to be smuggled into the Abbey under the thin disguise of *The Unknown Warrior*, thereby avoiding offence to anti-Popish feeling.

Undistinguished as the oath by St George has become, he has at any rate had the honour of outlasting all his peers. Where is there an Englishman who, mislaying his purse or his pipe, will threaten it in the name of St Anthony? or blackguarding a cobbler for making a bad repair to his boots will swear by the holy last of St Crispin that, if that cobbler does not do the job again properly, he will have half-a-pound of his own blunt brads forced down his lying throat? And whom has England got to match the Pope as a swearing-stock? Once in a public-house a young Italian and a middle-aged Londoner were arguing politics. The Italian paid a warm tribute to the Vatican and its works. 'Oh, to hell with the Pope!' remarked the Englishman. 'And to hell', replied the furious Italian, upsetting the glasses with a blow of his fist, 'and to hell with your Archbishop of Canterbury!' The Englishman swallowed the insult agreeably, but expostulated on the waste of good liquor.

Bound up with the taboo on the mention of God, of Heaven His throne, and Earth His footstool, and of all His other charges and minions, is the complementary taboo on the Devil, His ministers, and His prison-house. At one time the vain invocation of the Devil was an even more dangerous misdemeanour than the breach of the third Commandment. God, though He would not hold him guiltless who took His Name in vain, might forgive an occasional lapse; but the Devil, if ever called in professionally, would not fail to charge heavily for His visit. However, since the great Victorian day when an excited working-man came rushing out of the City church where Dean Farrar was preaching the gospel and shouted out to his friends at the public-house corner: 'Good news! old Farrar says there's no 'ell', the taboo has yearly weakened. 'That dreadful other place', as Christina respectfully called it in the death-bed scene of Butler's *Way of all Flesh*, is now seldom dwelt upon in the home pulpit, though the Law still formally insists on it as true because deterrent. One regretfully hears that the threat of hell's quenchless flames and the satyro-morphic view of Satan are now chiefly used for export purposes to Kenya and the Congo Basin, as a cement to the bonds of Empire.

There is no surer way of testing the current of popular religious opinion than by examining the breaches of the taboos in swearing. At the present day the First Person of the Trinity is not taken too seriously. 'O God!' has become only a low-grade oath and has crept into the legitimate vocabulary of the drawing-room and the stage. The Second Person, since the great evangelical campaigns of the last century overturned a despotism and inaugurated a spiritual republic, is far more firmly established. To swear by Jesus Christ is an oath with weight behind it. The Third Person is seldom appealed to, and makes a very serious oath, partly because of the Biblical warning that the sin against the Holy Ghost is the one unforgivable offence, and partly because the word *Ghost* suggests a sinister spiritual haunting. 'God' to the crowd is a benevolent or a laughable abstraction; Jesus Christ is a hero for whom it is possible to have a warm friendly feeling; but the Holy Ghost is a puzzle and to be superstitiously avoided.

From blasphemy and semi-blasphemy it is only a short step to secular irreverence. Many secular objects where they have become symbolic of deep-seated loyalties are held in the highest reverence by naval, military, and sporting society. The Crown and the Union Jack are for the governing classes enthroned beside the Altar and the Communion-cup. To call the smallest King's ship a 'boat', let alone a 'wretched tub' or 'lousy hencoop', is to invite broken ribs; to mistake a pack of hounds in full cry for a 'whole lot of howling dogs' is social suicide. The ingenious General G——r, so remarkable an artist in swearing that he must one day earn a paragraph in the revised *D.N.B.*, used this form of profanity with the happiest effect. Once, when inspecting the famous 'Z' Battery of the Royal Horse Artillery, he was dissatisfied with its response to his order 'Dismount!' He bellowed out: 'Now *climb back again*, you pack of consumptive little Maltese monkeys!' 'Z' Battery complained to Headquarters of this affront, and General G——r was in due course asked for his explanation and apology. He gave it briefly as follows:

'Sir,

I have the honour to report that, on the occasion to which I am referred, my order to dismount was obeyed in so slovenly a fashion that for the moment I was deceived. I concluded that I was actually assisting at a performance by a troop of little Maltese monkeys, amusing enough but crippled by disease. I tender my apologies to all ranks of 'Z' Battery for my mistake.

I have the honour to be, Sir,

Your obedient servant,

J. G——r.

Major-General.'

Besides these religious and semi-religious taboos there is a whole series forbidding the mention of any realistic danger or misfortune that may be lurking round the corner. So it is a greater personal offence to tell a taxi-man 'May your gears seize up and your tyres burst, and may you get pitched through your windscreen and break both legs against a lamp-post' than merely to ejaculate 'Blast your bleeding neck!' or 'Plague take you!' Instances of necks bleeding and divinely blasted are rarely met in General Hospitals, and England has been free from plague these two hundred years. To curse effectively one must invoke a reality or, at the least, a possibility. Any swearing that fails to wound the susceptibility of the person sworn at or of the witness to the oath, is mere play. Few people enjoy being sworn at, but there are no forms of humour more boring than guaranteed non-alcoholic substitutes for the true wine of swearing 'Great Jumping Beans!', 'Ye little fishes!', 'Snakes and ladders!', and 'Mind your step, you irregular old Pentagon!' If Sinclair Lewis has done nothing else in *Martin Arrowsmith*, he has at least nailed up as an abominable type Cliff Clawson, the medical student who indulged perpetually in this form of heartiness.

Among the governed classes one of the unforgivable words of abuse is 'bastard.' Bastardy is always a possibility, and savagely tormented whenever it appears; so that 'You bastard!' must be regarded as a definite allegation. Whereas in the governing classes there is far greater tolerance towards bastards, who often have noble or even royal blood in their veins, and who, under the courtesy title 'natural sons and daughters', have contributed largely to our ancestral splendours. On the other hand, the other common word in 'b.', which originally meant a Bulgarian heretic, but later implied 'one addicted to unnatural vice', is not a serious insult among the governed, who are more free from the homosexual habit. Dr Johnson rightly defined the word as 'a term of endearment among sailors'. Whereas in the governing classes the case is reversed. When some thirty years ago the word was written nakedly up on a club notice-board as a charge against one of its members, there followed a terrific social explosion, from which the dust has even now not yet settled. Had the accusation been 'Mr Wilde is a bastard', shoulders would merely have been shrugged at the noble lord's quixotic ill-temper. As it was . . .

And this brings us to the sex-taboo, from the violation of which abusive swearing draws its chief strength; mention even of the privy parts of the body is protected by a convention which has lost little of its rigidity since mid-Victorian times. The soldier, shot through the buttocks at Loos, who was asked by a visitor where he had been wounded, could only reply 'I'm so sorry, ma'am, I don't

know: I never learned Latin.' Public reference to
a man's navel, thighs, or arm-pits, even, is a serious
affront; from which the size of the 'breeches of
fig-leaves' tailored in Eden may be deduced. It is
difficult to determine how far this taboo is governed by the sense of reverence, and how far the
feeling is one of disgust and Puritanic self-hate.
But in any case the double function of the taboo'd
organs, the progenitive and excretory principals,
has confused the grammatic mind of civilization.

The words 'whore' and 'harlot' are among the
angriest properties of swearing in any class: in
the governed classes they are taken realistically, the
conditions of life being often so difficult under
industrialism that the temptation for a woman to
embark on this career is a serious one. In the
governing classes the accusation is one of aesthetic
coarseness: to have a *liaison* is excusable, and sometimes, if the lover chosen is sufficiently distin-
guished, even admirable; but the amateur status
must be strictly maintained in love as in sport. (It
may be noticed in passing that the word 'pro.' is a
deadly insult among Public School soccer players,
and the greatest compliment in village or waste-
ground football.) In no class, it is to be regretted,
does the accusation against a man that he consorts

with harlots rank as a serious insult, though 'pimp',
'ponce', and 'procurer' are ugly enough. For some
reason or other the hatred of cuckoldry has abated:
the very word is forgotten in popular talk; I would
welcome an explanation of this. But the prevalence
of 'unnatural vice' has added to the unforgivable
list the synonyms 'Nancy-boy', 'fairy', and 'poof'.
The chastity of sister or daughter has become a far
more serious consideration than the faithfulness of
a wife. When once the master of a Thames tug,
remonstrated with for fouling a pleasure-boat and
breaking an oar, leant over the rails and replied
hoarsely: 'Oh, I did, did I, Charley? And talking of
oars, 'ow's your sister?', he did so only in his de-
testation of the leisured classes and in confidence
of a clean get-away.[1]

[1] There is a great opportunity for ethnological research
in swearing of this sort. Why is it, for instance, that in
India the insult 'brother-in-law', carrying with it the im-
plication that a man has a liaison with his brother's wife, is
the one unforgivable insult (and the first word therefore
that the Imperialistic Englishman picks up thoughtlessly
for general conversational purposes)? Why in Egypt is a
man insulted best, paternally: 'O you father of sixty dogs!'
The answer will be found in a comparison of religions, the
Hindu laying most stress on the decencies of family life in a
large household, the Mohammedan on the passing down of
male perfection from father to son.

THE FUTURE OF SWEARING

Another serious abusive accusation in most classes is, fortunately enough, of venereal infection. 'Fortunately' because, though the stigma may tend in some cases to concealment of the disease, there have been times when infection has been considered a mark of manliness, a fashionable martyrdom. It was so considered on its first introduction into England, for Henry VIII was one of the first sufferers from the Neapolitan sickness; and it has been so considered in Central European military circles in quite recent times. This view was met even among young line-officers during the War. But the lasting and painful results of venereal disease are now generally realized, so 'pox-ridden' and 'clap-stricken' are daily gaining in offensiveness as epithets.

It is only a minor taboo that prevents reference to human excrement, but major swearing is strengthened by lavatory metaphors implying worthlessness or noisome disgust. Again, it is only a minor taboo that forbids mention of lice, fleas, and bugs. But the imputation of lousiness (except in the trenches, where it was a joke) carries serious implications with it; and the metaphorical 'You louse!' is ripe with hatred.

Now, the odd combinations that a witty and persistent mind could contrive from the breach of several of these taboos at once are far more numerous than appears at first sight. The lewd fellow who can go on swearing, without repetition, for a mere hour or more should not deserve the high popular esteem that he wins by the feat. Consider for a moment. It takes nine hours or more to exhaust the combinations of a full peal of church bells: then, while there are still so many taboos major or minor that a daring mouth can find to outrage, with such an ancient wealth of technical and associative matter to be excavated within each of these taboos, and so constant an enrichment of this ancient wealth by new pathological research, by religious sectarianism, and by the advance of our imperial frontiers; and while the effect of a discord played between the taboos which protect sacred objects and those which repress disgust or terror can be so shattering—well, then the recourse that most celebrated swearers take to foreign tongues or dialects must be considered a confession of imaginative failure.

Add to this positive foulmouthedness the art of negative swearing, and the thermodynamic entropy of the ingenious swearing-bout becomes even

more intense. The sequel to General G——r's in-
spection of 'Z' Battery is to the point here. He had
been privately given to understand that another
instance of abusive or foul language on parade
would cause him to lose his command. Then the day
came when he was not inspecting but being in-
spected, by the Commander-in-Chief of the Forces.
His brigade had assembled on the field of parade
half-an-hour before the C.-in-C. was expected, and
General G——r had posted a trumpeter at the gate
where the beflagged motor was expected to pull up.
The lad had been ordered to sound the call for
'Steady!' as soon as he saw the car approaching;
but, even if it did not arrive sooner, the call was in
any case to be given three minutes before the hour.
He was to watch the church clock. Time passed,
no car came, the call did not sound. Then the hour
chimed. Infuriated by this, the General set spurs
to his charger and thundered down to the gate.
Passion choked him, his face grew crimson. He
reined up by the terrified trumpeter and pointing
down at him with his finger, spoke in ogreish
tones:

'Oh, you naughty, naughty, naughty little trumpeter!' And at that moment under cover of a
hedge, for they had left their motor-cars on the

high road, up came the Commander-in-Chief and his staff on foot.

A physical training expert at Aldershot before the War knew the value of this negative form, the sarcastic Balaam's blessing where cursing is expected, the triviality more impressive than the thunder and whirlwind which went before it. Many of this staff-sergeant's best extempores have since been learned by rote and repeated by his pupils in season and out. Failing once after repeated positive efforts in swearing to induce in a squad the supple gymnastic style he expected, he moodily gave the 'Stand easy!' and beckoned the men up to hear a story. 'When I was a little nipper', he began, 'on my seventh birthday my dear old granny gave me a little box of wooden soldiers. Oh dear, you wouldn't imagine how pleased I was with them! I drilled them up and I drilled them down, and then one day I took them down to the seashore and lost them. Oh, you wouldn't believe how I cried! And when I came home to tea that night, late and blubbering, my dear old granny— her hair was white as snow and her soul whiter still—she says to me: "Little Archie, cheer up!" she says. "For God is good and one day you'll find your little wooden soldiers again." And Oh, good

God, she was right, *I have*. You wooden stiffs with the paint sucked off your faces!' And at another time, more simply and despairingly: 'Now men, I've done my best for you. I've sworn at you and sweated and coaxed you and it's all so much labour in vain. Now I say to you solemnly, solemnly, mind: "May the blessed Lord Jaycee take you into his merciful and perpetual keeping"; for I've done with you. Class; Dismiss!'

Of the necessity for swearing there is more than one opinion: large numbers both of the educated and the uneducated stand for the rigour of the taboo and for self-control: for them yea must always be yea, and nay, nay. Yet in practice they permit a few sterilized ejaculations, such as 'You silly beggar', which is the drawing-room synonym for the double b. of the street-corner; 'bother', 'blow', and 'dash' do service for 'damn', 'curse', and 'blast', which are just beyond the old-fashioned limit. For oaths there are 'By Jove!' 'By George!', and 'By Goodness!', and on comic occasions 'Odds-boddikins!' 'Strike me!', 'Swelp me Bob!', and 'By my halidom!' are dragged out, their blasphemy purged by the lapse of time. It is one of the curiosities of English that an oath by 'God's little bodies'—that is, by the Host—is a Christmas-annual jest, while 'Bloody', still stringently disallowed, is no more than an intensive of the same type as 'awfully', 'fearfully'; and originally quite polite. So Swift would write to inform Stella on May 28, 1711, that it was 'bloody hot walking to-day.' Another section of the community swears luxuriously, from anti-institutional conviction; but a middle course is, as usual, the most popular one: bad language is permitted only under extreme provocation, and even then must stop short of complicated invention.

Swearing as an art probably reached its highwater-mark in the late eighteenth century. The aristocracy was as careful in its protection of a corrupt Church as it was cynical about religion; and swearing as an assault on a coffee-house rival and introductory to a duel demanded a nice refinement of oratorical blasphemy; as the contemporary sermon demanded a nice refinement of oratorical eulogy. The Elizabethan Age may have been richer in far-fetched profanities and wild conceits than the Augustan Age, but swearing is an art that cannot trust to mere adventure for its success: it must have a controlled purpose, and always flourishes most strongly in a pure aristocracy, particularly a leisured town-dwelling aristocracy. The Elizabethan Age swore, it hardly knew how or why: and it was an excitable age with few settled convictions. The Augustan Age swore with deliberation and method, as clearly appears in Sheridan's *Rivals*:

Acres: 'If I can find out this Ensign Beverley, odds triggers and flints! I'll make him know the difference o't.'

Absolute: 'Spoken like a man! But pray, Bob, I observe you have got an odd kind of a new method of swearing.'

Acres: 'Ha! ha! you've taken notice of it— 'tis genteel, isn't it?— I didn't invent it myself though; but a commander in our militia, a great scholar I assure you, says that there is no meaning in the common oaths and that nothing but their antiquity makes them respectable—because, he says, the ancients would never stick to an oath or two, but would say, by Jove! or by Bacchus! or by Mars! or by Venus! or by Pallas! according to the sentiment; so that to swear with propriety, says my little major, the oath should be an echo to the sense; and this we call the *oath referential* or *sentimental swearing*—ha! ha! 'tis genteel, isn't it?'

Absolute: 'Very genteel and very new indeed!—and I daresay will supplant all other figures of imprecation.'

Acres: 'Ay, ay, the best terms will grow obsolete—Damns have had their day.'

There is no doubt that swearing has a definite physiological function; for after childhood relief in tears and wailing is rightly discouraged, and groans are also considered a signal of extreme weakness. Silence under suffering is usually impossible. The nervous system demands some expression that does not affect towards cowardice and feebleness and, as a nervous stimulant in a crisis, swearing is unequalled. It is a Saturnalian defiance of Destiny. Where rhetorical appeals to Fatherland, Duty, Honour, Self-respect, and similar idealistic abstractions fail, the well-chosen oath will often save the situation. At the beginning of the War, I was advised by peace-time soldiers never to swear at my men; and I was hurt by the suggestion that I could ever feel tempted to do so. But after putting the matter to a practical test in trench-warfare I changed my opinion, and later used to advise officer-cadets not to restrain their tongues altogether, for swearing had become universal, but to suit their language carefully to the occasion and to the type of men under their command, and to hold the heavier stuff in reserve for intense bombardments and sudden panics. For if, as may be questioned, it is a virtue to be a capable military leader, this virtue is not compatible in modern warfare with the virtue of the unqualified yea and the unintensified nay. Tristram Shandy's father, and his Uncle Toby, whose opinions had been formed some two hundred years before by trench warfare in the same district and curiously enough with the same battalion as I served with, had anticipated me here:

'Small curses, Dr Slop, upon great occasions', quoth my father, 'are but so much waste of our strength and soul's health to no manner of purpose.'

'I own it', replied Dr Slop.

'They are like sparrow-shot', quoth my Uncle Toby (suspending his whistling), 'fired against a bastion.'

'They serve', continued my father, 'to stir the

humours but to carry off none of their acrimony; for my own part, I seldom swear or curse at all— I hold it bad; but if I fall into it by surprise I generally retain so much presence of mind ("Right", quoth my Uncle Toby) as to make it answer my purpose, that is, I swear on till I find myself easy. A wise and just man however, would always endeavour to proportion the vent given to these humours, not only to the degree of them stirring within himself, but to the size and ill-intent of the offence upon which they are to fall.'

'Injuries come only from the heart' quoth my Uncle Toby.

But after this, Tristram Shandy, who was an Elizabethan born too late, treats of contemporary swearing and protests against the connoisseurs of swearing that they have pushed the formal critical control of swearing too far. He speaks of a gentleman, 'who sat down and composed, that is, at his leisure, fit forms of swearing suitable to all cases from the lowest to the highest provocation which could happen to him; which forms being well considered by him and such moreover as he could stand to, he kept them ever by him on the chimney-piece within his reach, ready for use.' Tristram

Shandy finds this practice far too academic. He asks no more than a single stroke of native genius and a single spark of Apollo's fire with it, and Mercury may then be sent to take the rules and compasses of correctness to the Devil. He says furthermore that the oaths and imprecations which have been lately 'puffed upon the world as originals' are all included by the Roman Church in its form of excommunication: that Bishop Ernulphus who formulated the exhaustive commination which he quotes (and which later the Cardinal used with such success on the Jackdaw of Rheims) has indeed brought categorical and encyclopaedic swearing to a point beyond which there can be no competition. He asks what is our modern 'God damn him!' beside Ernulphus':

May the Father who created man curse him!

May the Son who suffered for us curse him!

May the Holy Ghost who was given to us in baptism curse him!

May the Holy Cross, which Christ for our salvation triumphing over his enemies ascended, curse him!

May the holy and eternal Virgin Mary, mother of God, curse him!

May all the angels and archangels, principalities and powers, and all the heavenly armies curse him!

('Our armies swore terribly in Flanders' cried my Uncle Toby, 'but nothing to this. For my own part, I could not have a heart to curse my dog so.')

Tristram Shandy wrote at the beginning of the best period of English profanity (1760–1820). which owes a great debt to Voltaire and his fellow rationalists. The 'Zounds!', 'Icod!', 'Zoo dikers!', and 'Pox on you!' of a Squire Western were discarded by men of fashion, and the 'oath referential' of Acres, facetiously and indecently blasphemous, succeeded these: spreading their culture downwards and materially helping the national *morale* in the War-years that began the new century.

I do not think that Coleridge's distinction between the violent swearer who does not really mean what he says and the quiet swearer who swears from real malignity is an essential one. He writes in his apologetic preface to *Fire, Famine, and Slaughter*: 'The images, I mean, that a vindictive man places before his imagination will most often be taken from the realities of life: there will be images of

24

pain and suffering which he has himself seen in-
flicted on other men, and which he can fancy himself as inflicting on the object of his hatred. I will
suppose that we heard at different times two common sailors, each speaking of some one who had
wronged or offended him, that the first with ap-
parent violence had devoted every part of his adversary's body and soul to all the horrid phantoms
and fantastic places that even Quevedo dreamed of,
and this in a rapid flow of those outrageous and
wildly combined execrations which too often with
our lower-classes serve for escape-valves to carry
off the excess of their passions, as so much super-
fluous steam that would endanger the vessel if it
were retained. The other, on the contrary, with
that sort of calmness of tone which is to the ear
what the paleness of anger is to the eye, shall simply
say "If I chance to be made boatswain, as I hope I
soon shall, and can but once get that fellow under
my hand (and I shall be on the watch for him), I'll
tickle his pretty skin. I won't hurt him, oh, no! I'll
only cut the —— to the liver." I dare appeal to
all present which of the two they would regard as
the least deceptive symptom of deliberate malignity
—nay, whether it would surprise them to see the
first fellow an hour or two afterwards cordially

shaking hands with the very man the fractional parts of whose body and soul he had been so charitably disposing of; or even perhaps risking his life for him.'

No general distinction of motive can be made between swearers who adopt one or other of these methods. The art of one is that of the whirlwind boxer who comes bustling into the ring and excites admiration in the audience, and he hopes, fear in his opponent by a great display of unnecessary footwork and shoulder-shaking: the other is an old hand, who saves his strength and misleads his opponent, if he can, by pretended slowness and even by 'boxing silly', but after a few ingenuous leads, such as 'I'll tickle his pretty skin! I won't hurt him, oh no!' out comes the heavy right-to-jaw: 'I'll only cut the —— to the liver'; with telling effect. And Coleridge obscures the fact that to refuse to shake hands with a man in public, or, even more, to refuse to risk one's life for him, are breaches of social custom far more serious in male society than an oath.

Frequent swearing, then, is often, no doubt, the accompaniment of debauch, cruelty, and presumption, but, on the other hand, it is as often merely what the psychologists call the 'sublimation in fantasia of a practical anti-social impulse'; and what others call 'poor man's poetry'. But if the latter simile be permitted, it would seem that original poets are as rare in modern non-literary as they are in literary society. Occasionally in low life one hears a picturesque ancestral oath or an imaginative modern one coined by some true blasphemer and carefully stored by an admirer for his own use—'as in wild earth a Grecian vase'. But for the most part the dreary repetition of the two sexual mainstays of barrack-room swearing is the despair of the artist. This is a mechanical age, and even our swearing has been standardized.

The popular satire entitled simply *The Australian Poem* and satirizing the adjectival barrenness of the Australian Forces in the War, will be recalled:

> A sunburnt bloody stockman stood,
> And in a dismal, bloody mood
> Apostrophized his bloody cuddy:
> 'This bloody moke's no bloody good,
> He doesn't earn his bloody food,
> Bloody! Bloody! Bloody!'
>
> He leapt upon his bloody horse
> And galloped off, of bloody course.

The road was wet and bloody muddy:
It led him to the bloody creek;
The bloody horse was bloody weak,
Bloody! Bloody! Bloody!

He said 'This bloody steed must swim
The same for me as bloody him!'
The creek was deep and bloody floody
So ere they reached the bloody bank
The bloody steed beneath him sank—
The stockman's face a bloody study
Ejaculating Bloody! bloody! bloody!

Orderly-room charges of obscene and blasphemous language show a distressing sameness:

'Sir, the accused called me an x—ing y——' or
'Sir, the accused called me a y—ing x——'.

'And what have you to say for yourself, my man?'

'Well, sir, it was because the lance-corporal
called me a double x—ing y——, and I didn't
think it was right.'

The only novelty I remember in a long series of
these charges was: 'Sir, the accused used threatening and obscene language; his words were "Two
men shall meet before two mountains".'

Omne ignotum pro obsceno is the rule among the

uneducated. Mr W. H. Davies' odd story will be recalled. An old hedge-schoolmaster one day came as a stranger to the Inn in South Wales where the poet was drinking, and sat down at a corner table. Presently he cried out twice in a loud voice: 'Aristotle was the pupil of Plato.' After a moment's silence the men at the bar protested: 'Keep silence, you there!' Their wives caught their skirts tightly to them: 'We are respectable married women and did not come here to be insulted.' The publican threatened to throw the speaker out if he uttered any further obscenity. But the old man apologized in the acceptable formula: 'No offence intended; I am a stranger here'; and was forgiven. After long pondering on this story, I believe that I have got the clue. *Aristotle's Works* (with illustrations) is sold in every rubber-shop in London and Cardiff, in company with other more obviously erotic publications. I have never had the courage to buy a copy and see what is wrong with the philosopher; but I suspect the worst. And certainly 'Aristotle' to the public-house mind is known only in the rubber-shop context. But I can testify to a man having been thrown out of the Empire Lounge some years ago for calling a barmaid a 'maisonette'. ('Indeed you're wrong; I'm an honest woman.')

Of swearing-duels little is now heard. They used to be frequent, tradition says, in the good old days when public-houses kept open all night and beer was more strongly brewed: alas, I can find little historical matter to indicate what was the technique and range of this popular art at its Dickensian prime.[1] But at least the palm of victory does not always seem to have gone to the most resonant or strong-chested artist. Often, as in jujitsu, a man's own strength is turned against him. It is recorded that once in the City an Admiral's brougham was obstructed by a coster's barrow and that the Admiral improved the occasion by a very heavy and god-damnatory flow of abuse. The coster let him have his say; but as he paused for breath remarked cheerfully: 'If you was better house-trained, Jackie, I'd take you home for a pet.'

I am informed that the legal view of abusive swearing is that, unless calculated to cause a breach of the peace, it is no offence. So that it is just possible to call a man a blasted fool in public. On the other hand, there is an offence in calling him plain

[1] Though swearing in fashionable society began to decline as an art about the same time as the wig disappeared, it flourished among the lower classes for fifty years longer.

and unqualified fool: that constitutes a libel and a penalty can be exacted.

Of American swearing I am not qualified to write, but I understand that in vulgar life the convention there is somewhat different. 'Bastard' and 'son of a bitch' are friendly terms of reproach. This recalls the experience of an American tourist, Mrs Beech, who was staying in Paris after the War. An elderly Frenchman who was introduced to her greeted her cordially: 'Ah, Mrs Beech, Mrs Beech, you are one of ze noble muzzers who gave so many sons to ze War.'

Might not a useful addition be made to this *To-day and To-morrow* series, by some worthier, more energetic, and more scholarly hand than mine? To be called *Lars Porsena; or The Future of Swearing*. Lars Porsena, if we may trust Lord Macaulay, was more fortunate than ourselves: he had no less than nine gods to swear by, and every one of them in Tarquin's time was taken absolutely seriously. How would the argument run? On the lines perhaps of the following synopsis:

The imaginative decline of popular swearing under industrial standardization and since the popular Education Acts of fifty years ago; the possibility that swearing under an anti-democratic régime will recover its lost prestige as a fine art; following the failure of the Saints and Prophets, and the breakdown of orthodox Heaven and Hell as supreme swearing-stocks, the rich compensation offered by newer semi-religious institutions, such as the 'League of Nations' and 'International Social-ism', and by superstitious objects such as pipes, primroses, black-shirts, and blood-stained banners; the chances of the eventual disappearance of the sex-taboo and of the slur on bastardy, but in the near future the intentional use of Freudian symbols as objurgatory material; the effect on swearing of the gradual spread of spiritistic belief, of new popu-lar diseases such as botulism and sleepy-sickness, of new forms of chemical warfare, of the sanction which the Anglican Church is openly giving to contraception, thereby legitimizing the dissocia-tion of the erotic and progenitive principles and of feminism challenging the view that hard swearing is a proof of virility. Research would be suggested on the variations of taboo in different English-speaking lands[1] on the alliterative emphasis and

[1] A man charged recently at Hoxton with using language calculated to make a breach of the peace complained that at

rhythm of swearing, on the maximum nervous reaction that can be got from a normal subject by combinations and permutations of the oath, the results to be recorded on a highly sensitive kymograph. Finally this valuable and carefully documented work might treat of the prospects of Pure Swearing; by which is not meant sterilized swearing or 'Cliff Clawsonism', but *Swearing without a practical element, with only a musical relation between the images it employs. Swearing of universal application and eternal beauty,* following the recent sentimental cult for Pure Poetry.

'But how is this?' the reader asks 'Isn't what I'm reading called *Lars Porsena, or the Future of Swearing*'. I apologize for a little joke, somewhat resembling those advertisements in *Snappy Bits*, which promise erotic delights to any schoolboy who will send five shillings and a statement that he is not a minor: only to fob him off with badly printed photographs of classical paintings and statuary—for to send indecent matter by post is

---

Bethnal Green, where he lived, he could have said all that and more with impunity. He suggested a swearing-directory for the London district, which should indicate what you might say there.

illegal. No doubt the Chic-Art Publishing Company would not object to dealing more faithfully with its clients if it could, and perhaps the delight of expectation is worth the ensuing disappointment of only getting the Venus of Milo and a Rubens or two to gloat over. But though a joke is a joke, this volume goes as far as it decently can in containing at least a few classically draped forecasts and an honest inquiry into the taboos which prevent publication of the real *Lars Porsena*. And, anyhow this is nearest to a *Lars Porsena* that will ever be published. For as soon as there is sufficient weakening of the taboos to permit an accurate and detailed account of swearing and obscenity, then, by that very token, swearing and obscenity can have no future worth prophesying about, but only a past more or less conjectural because undocumented.

Though Samuel Butler's definition of 'Nice People' as 'people with dirty minds' can be misunderstood by critics who refuse to differentiate between the humorously obscene and the obscenely obscene, I like it. No nice person is uncritical; and yet we are all hedged round with an intricate system of taboos against 'obscenity'. To consent uncritically to the taboos, which are often grotesque, is as foolish as to reject them uncritically. The nice person is one who good-humouredly criticizes the absurdities of the taboo in good-humoured conversation with intimates; but does not find it necessary to celebrate any black masses as a proof of his emancipation from it. This book is written for the Nice People. Then, though it is in its first intention a detached treatise on swearing and obscenity, it cannot claim a complete innocence of obscenity, while consenting to the publishers' limitations of what is printable and what is not. Observe with what delicacy I have avoided and still avoid writing the words x—— and y——, and dance round a great many others of equally wide popular distribution. I have yielded to the society in which I move, which is an obscene society: that is, it acquiesces emotionally in the validity of the taboo, while intellectually objecting to it. I have let a learned counsel go through these pages with a blue pencil and strike through paragraph after paragraph of perfectly clean writing. My only self-justification is that the original manuscript is to be kept safe for a more enlightened posterity in the strong-room of one of our greater libraries.

Horace is my idea of a characteristically obscene man. An immoderate liking for his poems is, I believe, a sure proof of obscenity in any person.

Catullus, on the other hand, was not obscene: he had greater self-respect. Witness his:

> Caeli, Lesbia nostra, Lesbia illa
> Illa Lesbia quam Catullus unam
> Plus quam se atque suos amavit omnes.
> Nunc in quadriviis et angiportis
> Glubit magnanimos Remi nepotes.

Where 'Glubit' by self-disgust and by the bitter irony of the 'magnanimos Remi nepotes' leaves obscenity looking foolish. The 'Long Man of Cerne' carved out in chalk on the Dorset Downs is not obscene in the real sense that the modern Cinema is obscene with its sudden blackings-out at the crisis of sexual excitement.

When a future historian comes to treat of the social-taboos of the nineteenth and twentieth centuries in a fourteen-volume life-work, his theories of the existence of an enormous secret-language of bawdry and an immense oral literature of obscene stories and rhymes known, in various degrees of initiation, to every man and woman in the country, yet never consigned to writing or openly admitted as existing, will be treated as a chimerical notion by the enlightened age in which he writes. As Sir James Frazer took, as the text for his inquiries, the Golden Bough legend of Aricia and the primitive ceremonies there surviving until Imperial times, so this new Sir James may take *The Bottom Legend* recorded by a contemporary historian Roberts as his text. As follows:

'Shortly before the "Great War for Civilization" (the indecisive conflict, 1914–1918, between rival European confederations to decide which was to have the right of defining Civilization) there was a student of Oxford University famous for his "practical joking." He is said to have been one of the rare persons of the day to whom a peculiar licence was given for such "practical joking" and for deriding the most sacred taboos of the time. It was he who first defiled a local altar, "The Martyrs' Memorial", by climbing to the very summit at night-time and planting a chamber-pot—a stringently taboo'd vessel—on the cross which crowned it. The civic authorities had great difficulty in removing this scandalous object, because climbing the Memorial was no easy feat, and the chamber-pot, being made of enamelware and not, as was first thought, of porcelain, could not be dislodged by rifle fire. On another occasion, this same student is said to have impersonated an African potentate and, with a suite of disguised companions, to have been officially welcomed with a Royal Salute aboard a battleship of the English Navy, and to have aggravated this quasi-blasphemous performance (for the Fleet was a religious institution of greater dignity and efficiency than the Church itself) by the bestowal of medals on the ship's officers.

'But the most interesting breach of taboo with which he is credited was a dinner-party which he gave at a Cathedral town in the Midlands. He spent over a year, and a great deal of money, in scraping acquaintance under an assumed name with every person in the town whose surname contained the syllable "bottom": Ramsbottom, Longbottom, Sidebottom, Winterbottom, Higginbottom, Whethambottom, Bottomwhetham, Bottomwallop, Bottomley, and plain Bottom; he insinuated himself into the friendship of every one of these families, but separately, without allowing them to meet in his presence, until finally he was able to invite them all together to a huge dinner-party at his hotel. When each name in turn had been announced by a particularly loud-voiced hotel-servant, he withdrew, promising to return in a few minutes, and begging them to begin dinner without him. The meal consisted merely of rump-steak, and the host was already in a railway train, riding swiftly towards London, and leaving no address.

THE FUTURE OF SWEARING

'This story is regarded by Roberts and others as a most amusing one, though the point of the joke will need explaining to readers of this thirtieth century.

'Apparently "bottom" was the common equivalent, in the secret language which I postulate, of the word "buttocks". Now, among primitive peoples *no man will utter common words which coincide with or merely resemble in sound taboo'd names*, and, though the twentieth century refused to admit itself primitive, we cannot now understand on what grounds this refusal could have been plausibly justified. The principle I have italicized is a direct quotation from a contemporary treatise on taboo. The author, whose name has been lost with the title-page of the unique copy in the Jerusalem Library, was only able to state this principle in the case of the South African Zulus and other savage tribes; but there is little doubt in my mind that the point of the joke lay in the sensitivity of the Bottom families to the obscene connotations of their name. That the buttocks should have been taboo'd is a surprising idea, but apparently a morbid prolongation of the lavatory-taboo accounts for it: or so Mannheim holds. The Bottom names either had no original connexion with the buttocks as in *Bottomwallop*, which is a geographical name, or, as in *Longbottom*, they were inherited from an age when the taboo had not yet hardened. Be that as it may, the unfortunates who were born at this period to a name containing the taboo'd syllable were in a quandary. If they changed their names by Deed Poll, the expense and embarrassment would be considerable. Yet not to change meant that they would continue to be aware of repressed snickering wherever they went beyond the immediate circle of their friends. Most of them, therefore, changed the spelling merely from "Bottom" to "Botham", and thus thought to circumvent the taboo. Indeed, as Roberts tells the story, the Bottom-guests were all disguised as Bothams or Bottomes. One family, the Sidebottoms or Sidebothams, went so far as to pronounce their name "Siddybotaam" and in Bigland's *Life and Times of H. Bottomley* (1954) there is mention of one of these "Siddybotaams" to whom Bottomley (a famous practical joker) is said to have introduced himself as "H. Bumley, Esq.", "bum" being a common, but strongly taboo'd, shortening of "bottom".

'Now, the secret language, which was generally known as "smut"—possibly the idea of defilement is latent in this word, since another synonym was "The Dirty Talk" or "The Foul Language" was so rich in its vocabulary, and drew so copiously on the legitimate language for secret obscene usages of common words, that the greatest ingenuity was needed in legitimate speech to avoid the appearance of obscenity. Thus so common a word as "bottom" meaning a *base*, a *bed*, a *fundament*, a *cause*, owing to its use in smut as an equivalent for "buttocks", could never be used in the legitimate language in any context where a *double entendre* might be understood. The word "parts" becoming a synonym in Smut of the organs of generation had to be used with great care, and these are merely two isolated instances of a principle so strong that when two persons who had been initiated into the third or fourth degree of the secret language began a conversation, practically not a single phrase could be used by them without this *double entendre*, causing hysterical laughter. *And not merely the names themselves but any words that sound like them are scrupulously avoided, and other words used in their place. A custom of this sort, it is plain, may easily be a potent agent of change in language, for, where it prevails to any considerable extent, many words must constantly become obsolete and new ones spring up.*

'This is a quotation from the same anonymous ethnologist, who is here discussing the taboos in

Melanesia and Australia on the mention of the names of certain relatives, whether dead or alive, but it also explains many linguistic changes in the vocabulary of the nineteenth, twentieth, and twenty-first centuries: for instance, the constant out-of-dating of popular equivalents to the words "whore" and "harlot" which being Biblical alone remained in constant use as pure descriptive terms; and the disappearance from common use of the phrase "a man of parts", meaning "a man of great attainments", and the phrase "he (or she) has no bottom", meaning that the person referred to has no stability of character. It will be seen that this furtive language must have had a great influence on the legitimate language.

'For confirmation of my theory of the indecency of the word "bottom" see Boswell's *Life of Doctor Johnson* under the date of 1781:

> Talking of a very respectable author he told us a curious circumstance in his life, which was, that he had married a printer's devil.
>
> *Reynolds*: 'A printer's devil, sir! Why I thought a printer's devil was a creature with a black face and in rags.'
>
> *Johnson*: 'Yes, sir. But I suppose he had her

face washed and put clean clothes on her. (Then looking very serious and very earnest.) And she did not disgrace him; the woman had a bottom of good sense.' The word *bottom* thus introduced was as ludicrous when contrasted with his gravity, that most of us could not forbear tittering and laughing; though I recollect that the Bishop of Killaloe kept his countenance with perfect steadiness, while Miss Hannah More slyly hid her face behind a lady's back who sat on the same settee with her. His pride could not bear that any expression of his should excite ridicule, when he did not intend it; he therefore resolved to assume and exercise despotick power, glanced sternly around and called out in a strong tone, 'Where's the merriment?' Then collecting himself and looking aweful to make us feel how he could impose restraint, and as it were searching his mind for a still more ludicrous word, he slowly pronounced 'I say the *woman* was *fundamentally* sensible' as if he had said 'Hear this now and laugh if you dare!' We all sat composed as at a funeral.

'*New words sprang up everywhere, like mushrooms in the night. . . . The mint of words was in the hands*

*of the old women of the tribe, and whatever term they
stamped with their approval and put into circulation,
was immediately accepted without a murmur by high
and low alike, and spread like wildfire through every
camp and settlement of the tribe.*

'This is our ethnologist, again, on the Paraguay
Indians: but he does not enlighten us as to who
held the word-mint of Smut in his own country. It
seems probable that the Stock-Exchange was re-
sponsible for a greater part of the new coinages, that
from the Stock-Exchanges they spread to the big
business houses, and were distributed by the commercial travellers to the provinces; but the close
connection of the Stock-Exchange with the Turf
made the bookmakers also useful disseminators of
the new coinages. A smutty story or a new word-
coinage seems to have been, with whisky-and-soda,
the usual ceremonial confirmation of a big business
deal or the laying of a bet. Other mints of greater
or less importance were the major Universities, the
Inns of Court, and the Military Academies.

'The composition of smutty rhymes, chiefly in a
strict five-line verse-form, known as the "Limerick",
with the conventional beginning "There once was
a . . .", was one of the chief occupations of these

44

high-priests of Smut, and two or three at least of the legitimate poets famous at the end of the twentieth century are known to have added largely to the common stock of tradition.

'Even in our enlightened times, the sex-taboo and lavatory-taboo linger to a certain extent, owing to the natural reserve men and women feel about these functions. The lavatory-taboo still survives with us at meal-times, but we find it difficult to understand the extraordinary customs to which the morbid enlargement of this natural reserve led. For instance, the playwright Hogg records that not only was it considered obscene for a man to show a woman the way to the lavatory, but that even man to man, or woman to woman, an evasive phrase had to be used: "Would you care to wash your hands?" "Have you been shown the geography of the house"? nor would even intimate friends consent to notice each other if one of them was emerging from the lavatory or entering it; and, if this was the first meeting of the day, would greet each other half-a-minute later on un-taboo'd ground with every pretence of novelty and surprise. If a woman had a slight contusion on the breast, it was considered most obscene to mention it directly, but tender inquiries would be made after "your poor side", "your injured shoulder". So our anonymous ethnologist, in a caustic account of the idea of virgin-birth among primitive tribes, is forced to write:

> '*Nana, the mother of Attis, was a virgin who conceived by putting a ripe almond in her bosom.*

'The curious alternation of prudishness and prurience in the social life of the time makes strange reading. On one hand were to be found sexual extravagances so fantastic as to be quite unintelligible to-day even to modern physiologists, on the other such delicacy of feeling that in some classes of Society the word "leg" was actually taboo'd and we have it on the authority of the social historian Gilett Burgess that in Boston in the 1880's it was considered necessary to clothe the naked legs or "limbs" of tables with white cotton pantaloons. Until the decade following the "Great War for Civilization", the young women of the English moneyed and middle classes lived what was called "very sheltered lives": which meant that, in the name of modesty, they were left to find out for themselves the simplest facts about the sexual mechanism. These facts, probably owing to a morbidity induced by the lavatory-taboo, they seem to have been frequently unable to grasp. Literature gave them little clue, owing to the custom of writing one part of the body when another was meant; and the use of words like "kiss", "embrace", and "hug", as synonyms for the sexual act confused them so completely that in a majority of cases they were married without having the vaguest idea of what really happens between man and woman, or how babies are born, and the suddenness of the realization frequently caused nervous shock and even madness. The young men, on the other hand, by the time that they came to marry, usually had had such a fantastic experience of sex-life among the professional "harlots" of a lower social class that it was most rare for a satisfactory sex-adjustment to be made between them and their wives; and it is computed that at least nine marriages out of ten were completely wrecked before the "honeymoon" was over.

Between 1919 and 1929 there was a marked relaxing of the sex-taboos among the educated classes: in art-exhibitions though not in public art-galleries, painting of female nudes in which the pubic hair was represented were for the first time admitted. There were also great changes during this decade in the fashion of women's dresses. Skirts, which hitherto had hidden the ankles, now revealed the knees; and 'evening dresses' were worn, we are told, 'without any backs', though it is conjectured that the buttocks were still covered. 'Bathing-dresses', garments worn by both sexes, even when actually swimming in the water, became less voluminous, and the use of 'bathing-stockings' by women was discontinued. There is record of a novelist James Joyce, whose works, though published in a foreign country, probably France, were smuggled into England, openly read and even regarded as 'modern classics' by a literary minority: Joyce appears to have defied all taboos in his writing, and it is a pity that the Universal-Fascismo combination of 1929 succeeded in destroying every copy of his most famous work *Ulysses*, which would have been a mine of information for our present inquiry.

'For the rest of the century the taboos continued almost as strongly enforced as in the period preceding the War.

'Indeed, Fascismo did its work so thoroughly that only tantalizing scraps remain of those few records of Smut made in the post-War decade, and the post-Fascismo records are not particularly helpful. By the edict of 1930 the talk of Smut became a capital offence, and when in 1998 the regulation was relaxed, the tradition had become almost extinct. It is now, therefore, impossible to suggest accurately what were the different degrees of initiation of which Hogg speaks, nor how the different dialects of Smut—Garage Smut, Club Smut, Mess Smut, School Smut—varied. But our knowledge of preceding centuries is no less scanty. We have no critical apparatus for filling in the lacunae in Marcus Clarke's account of convict obscenity in his Australian novel *For the Term of his Natural Life*, or in Benjamin Disraeli's account of industrial obscenity in the 1830's given in *Sybil*; nor can we supplement Alec Waugh's hints of Public School obscenity in his *Loom of Youth* (1917). The poets were as timorous as the novelists. James Stephens records a 'shebeen' curse of the 1920 period:

The lanky hank of a she in the inn over there
Nearly killed me for asking the loan of a glass of
  beer:
May the Devil grip the whey-faced slut by the
  hair
And beat bad manners out of her skin for a year.

That parboiled imp with the hardest jaw you
  will see

49

> On virtue's path and a voice that would rasp the
>   dead.. . .
>
> . . . May she marry a ghost and bear him a
>   kitten, and may
> The High King of Glory permit her to get the
>   mange;

but it is most unlikely that this is a faithful example
of the swearing of that day. It is known that swearing in the War[1] was of a very violent character, but
not a trace of it, beyond an occasional *damn* or
bloody, occurs in Siegfried Sassoon's otherwise very
realistic war-poems. Contemporary newspaper
reports of divorce-proceedings are known to have
been rigorously cut: such euphemisms were em-
ployed as 'a certain condition', 'a certain posture',
'a certain organ', 'a certain unnatural vice', so that
it is difficult to know why such interest in these
cases was shown by the readers of the newspapers,
unless they were possessed of that primitive intui-
tion which the savages in our own Central African
reservations still to some measure display.

[1] Field records that a party of deaf and dumb children
were in 1918 taken to a cinema-show called The Somme
Film, and had to be taken away because of the 'bad language'
on the screen.

THE FUTURE OF SWEARING

'Two cases are known of a whole edition (150,000 copies) of a daily newspaper having to be destroyed because of a breach of the taboo which escaped the proof-reader. Both are recorded by Brunel in his *Recent Press History* 1928, but he mentions no names and does not explain the matter in great detail:

> The whole country edition of one of our leading dailies had on one occasion to be suppressed because of a one-word change made in a leading article by a printer who was under notice of discharge: the alteration was made after the proofs had been passed. The offending passage originally read:
>
> 'I saw in a Tory journal the other day (23 Jan, 1882) a note of alarm in which they said: "Why, if a tenant farmer is elected for the North Riding, the farmers will be a political power to be reckoned with. The speaker then said *he* felt inclined for a bit of farming. I think that is very likely (Laughter).'

The second occasion was this: an evening paper injudiciously printed a letter on the disorganization of the London traffic without observing the signature: which was R. Supward. The edition had to be destroyed at the cost of several thousand pounds.

'It is a pity that Brunel has left us in the dark about the obscene connotation of *Supward*: perhaps it stands for "Bedward", supper being the preliminary to bed, and *bed* being a taboo'd word. But this is only a conjecture. Nor do we know what action would have been taken in the matter by the Censor, an official in whose hands the avenging of all broken taboos lay, had the mistake not been noticed in time; but certainly it must have been a serious one, a heavy fine or a temporary suppression of publication. It seems possible, however, that it was not merely fear of the Censorship which preserved the strength of these taboos: they were sometimes valued on their own account by men and women of otherwise considerable intellectual force. Thus, while our ethnologist writes of the primitive savage "so tightly bound" by taboos of another variety that he "scarcely knows which way to turn", he is careful to express "the enormous debts which we owe to the savage," and the context makes it plain that chief among these debts are the ideas of "decency" and "morals" in their most fantastic development. Johnstone, an essayist of this period, has a passage which it would not be out of place to quote here:

THE FUTURE OF SWEARING

But I cannot describe the awful look of horror which I remember in the eyes of middle-aged women of the pre-War decade when they uttered the word *décolletée* ("with a low-necked dress cut almost to the bosom") or the embarrassment still shown by the young schoolmistress or even the young schoolmaster in the Divinity lesson, should the innocent question be piped: 'Please, teacher, what does "whoremonger" mean?'

'The ethnologist from whom we have been quoting gives us the most authoritative of all surviving late nineteenth-century accounts of the superstitions, taboos, and magic of earlier primitive peoples; but what impresses us most now besides the lucidity of the argument is the elaborate care with which, as we have seen, the author has consented to the sexual and religious taboos of his own society and the great number also of literary and academic superstitions in which his accounts of savage superstitions are dressed. Though clearly a great force in the contemporary movement for the breaking of taboos that had outlasted their use, he never makes a direct attack upon them. It may indeed be said that he clings to the very superstition which he records among primitive tribes, that to dispatch the tribal god by indirect means is not blasphemy in the first degree: that is, he treats facetiously the beliefs and ceremonies of almost every religion but that of contemporary English Protestantism, but points out the common resemblances and leaves the reader to take the inevitable step. For instance, he derides the claims of priests to divine revelation, the doctrines also of Immaculate Conception, Redemption of Sins, the Real Presence in the Sacrament, the Resurrection of a slain God, the transference of evil spirits to goats and swine, but only derides them in religions earlier than Christianity and, therefore, "superstitious". Though heretics within Christianity are ridiculed by him for having claimed divinity for themselves, the divinity of Jesus Christ is nowhere directly impugned: who is permitted to have been immaculately conceived, to have cast out devils, taken over the burden of human sin, and risen again. He is allowed a capital F as Founder of Christianity, and the Virgin Mary is written of with traditional tenderness and reverence.

'As regards literary and academic superstitions, our author's faithfulness to contemporary literary ritual is such that even pedants who recognized the dangerous tendencies of his theory were forced to applaud the beauty of his style with its heavy rhetorical ornaments, its numerous and unnecessary quotations from the duller poets, and its most careful avoidance of repetition even where repetition is necessary for the clarity of the argument. For example, he cannot bring himself to write plainly:

> Every province had the tomb and mummy of its dead god. The mummy of Osiris was at Mendes, the mummy of Anhouri at Thinis, the mummy of Toumon at Heliopolis.

He must dress it up as:

> The mummy of Osiris was to be seen at Mendes, Thinis boasted of the mummy of Anhouri, and Heliopolis rejoiced in the possession of that of Toumon;

and in chapters where analogous customs of many tribes have to be catalogued and compared, this fear of repeating the same phrase soon fidgets the reader so much that he forgets what he is reading about. Our author also feels the academic necessity for an occasional platitude in the ancient 'moral progress' superstition to round off an over-argumentative chapter; it seems to weigh as heavily upon him as the necessity of sacrificing black wallabies (or were they black cockatoos?) in time of drought weighed on the Australian blackfellow. He writes:

> The fallacy of such a belief is plain to us; yet perhaps the self-restraint which these and the like beliefs, vain and false as they are, have imposed on mankind has not been without its utility in bracing and strengthening the breed. For strength of character in the race as in the individual consists mainly in the power of sacrificing the present to the future, of disregarding the immediate temptations of ephemeral pleasure for the more distant and lasting sources of satisfaction. The more the power is exercised, the higher and stronger becomes the character; till the height of heroism is reached in men who renounce the pleasures of life itself for the sake of keeping or winning for others, perhaps in distant ages, the blessing of freedom and truth.

'*Braced and strengthened* with this belief *vain and false* as it may be, that the *blessings of freedom and truth* are *kept and won*, that the *character of the race and of the individual* becomes *higher and stronger* by such *self-restraint and sacrifice*, he is particularly careful of the ephemeral temptation to abuse the sex-taboo.

'While he speaks with bantering condescension of the poor savage who used the navel-cord and severed genitals of his relatives for the magic purposes of agriculture, the language he chooses is blamelessly scientific. In other words, he gives himself the privilege of the priests who may treat of the holy mysteries plainly, but in the sacred language and not in the vernacular. Or else, as one of the people, he is exquisitely circumlocutory in his accounts of primitive orgies:

'A striking feature of the worship of Osiris as a god of fertility was the coarse but expressive symbolism by which this aspect of his nature was presented to the eye, not merely of the initiated, but of the multitude. . . . At Philae the dead god is portrayed lying on his bier in an attitude which indicates in the plainest way that even in death his generative virtue was not extinct, but only suspended. . . . One may conjecture that in this paternal aspect. . . .

And shortly afterwards, he gravely wonders at the

57

savage dread of menstrual blood. Klein, in one of his essays, suggests that the whole book is satiric in intention, and in a private letter has charged me with having no sense of humour because I refuse to read it in this way. But I prefer for once to have no sense of humour.'

To conclude, swearing as an art is at present in low water. National passion seldom runs high, invention is numbed, and there is no appeal of a politico-religious nature which will meet everywhere with the same respect. The only taboo strong enough to be worth breaking is the sexual one, and swearing shows every sign of continuing standardized on that basis for some time. It may be that 'bastard', and similar words, may gradually creep into legitimate speech, but only because obscener equivalents have been found.

The only really effective form of swearing that I know is this: Suppose you quarrel violently with a fellow-traveller in a crowded railway-carriage, perhaps about opening windows or the disposition of luggage. You get worsted. 'Very well', you say, with a sigh, 'have it your own way.' 'By the way', you add, with a peculiar intensity, 'I happen to know that in three weeks' time you will have a dangerous illness.' If the quarrel has been very violent, you may even sentence your adversary to death.

You have not used obscene or threatening language, or expressed a wish that your adversary should suffer. You have not used God's name. If you had done any of these things you would not only be putting yourself in danger of prosecution and alienating the sympathy of the other travellers, but you would further be weakening the effect of your curse. 'God damn you', says Jones to Brown. Brown says to himself: 'Good; Jones is thoroughly annoyed with me, and afraid to do anything but curse.' And Brown considers himself on good terms with God, and cannot imagine the latter being influenced by any angry petitions of Jones. But 'You will have a dangerous illness in three weeks' time' is a different matter. For all the traveller knows, you may be a specialist, giving a free diagnosis of his condition. Pride will keep him from asking you on what grounds you said what you did. If he does ask, he cannot force a reply from you without assault. Keep silence for the rest of the journey, and watch his nerves gradually go. He is pinned in that corner-seat with you opposite him: he has no refuge from your curse because he does not understand it. The more often he tells himself that he should pay no attention to you, the more irritating will be the superstitious reactions. When eventually you part, he takes the curse home with him—not your curse, but his own. For this is an individualistic age: the community has little power over the individual, and, if you would curse effectively, it must not be done in the name of the community or the formula of the community. You must put it into your adversary's mind to curse himself with his own fears. 'Injuries only come from the heart' quoth my Uncle Toby.

A final word and a most important one. No critic of this essay will be satisfied unless fuller mention is made of James Joyce's *Ulysses* than has here been given. But they must remain unsatisfied. Though *Ulysses* could be studied as a complete manual of contemporary obscenity, such a study will get no encouragement here. It is true that *Ulysses* is forbidden publication in England as indecent and that it contains more words classified by law as indecent than any other work published this century; but on the other hand it also contains more obscure poetic and religious references than any other work published this century and the choice of language in the blameless passages is as scholarly as Mr Sainsbury's and as English as Charles Doughty's. So far from being a work of merely pornographic intention or even a serious work given the pornographic sugar-coating that Rabelais gave his politico-philosophic pills, it is a deadly serious work in which obscenity is anatomized as it has never been anatomized before. To call Joyce obscene is like calling the Shakespeare of the *Sonnets* lustful: true, both have had the intimate experiences that their writing implies, but Joyce has brought himself as far beyond obscenity as Shakespeare got beyond the lust of which he makes frank confession. Bloom, gross obscenity incarnate, is presented in *Ulysses* directly without the prejudice of tenderness or harshness. Stephen Daedalus whose early history had been given (semi-autobiographically) in *A Portrait of the Artist as a Young Man* is presented as a type of the over-sophisticated intellectual, a poet who has failed as a poet because he is unable to find any strong enough reality to make foundation for his poetry. In the contemporary religious and literary scene, though a man of strong natural religious feelings and great literary capacity, he finds only emptiness. Irish nationalist politics are no better. The only life that has any appearance of reality to him is the obscene life as lived by Bloom, the middle-aged married commercial traveller and by Mulligan, a forceful young medical student who lodges with Daedalus. Daedalus, who makes his living by schoolmastering in an old-fashioned school, is philosophically inclined to the obscene life because Bloom and Mulligan, who live it seriously, are in this respect at least superior to the priests, the schoolmasters, and the little Celtic-Twilight poets (Joyce himself began as one) whose lives have no such absorption in a ruling idea. Yet as a sensitive person Daedalus is utterly repelled by the badness and rankness which obscenity exudes; and in the spiritual conflict between an artist's love of reality and an artist's hatred of obscenity the plot of the book lies. The only character in the book with whom Daedalus has a strong natural sympathy is his father, the only one man who is able to harmonize religion, politics, and obscenity into something like an artistic reality. Old Daedalus swears admirably. Though most of his oaths are on the censored list there is no disgust stirred by them:

A tall black-bearded figure, bent of a stick, stumping round the corner of Elvery's elephant-house showed them a curved hand on his spine.

THE FUTURE OF SWEARING

'In all his pristine beauty,' Mr Power said. Mr Daedalus looked after the stumping figure and said mildly:

'The devil break the hasp of your back!'

But Stephen has a bitter quarrel with his father since his mother's death, and anyhow finds no sympathy in him for the intellectual sophistication which is one of the chief causes of unrest. The book rises to a scream of dreadful pain when we come on Stephen drunk in Mabbot Street in company with Bloom, a bawd-mistress, and several harlots, two English private soldiers, and a whole fantastic crowd of the imaginary characters of Stephen's brain: dying away in a monstrously droned account of the trivialities of lust and obscenity to which early middle-age has brought Bloom and his wife.

It is quite right that *Ulysses* should be censored, since its chief public in England could at the best of times be only an obscene one: and it is not an obscene book, but on the contrary perhaps the least obscene book ever published: that is why it is censored. And there is every reason why Shakespeare's sonnets should be censored at the same time, and more strictly, because the public even blinds its eyes to the painful history that the sequence gives and makes it 'extravagant flattery of a patron' or an 'academic exercise.' Joyce is read as obscene instead of successfully past obscenity: Shakespeare instead of being read as past lust is not even read as lusting.

NOTE TO NEW EDITION

Many authorities on swearing and improper language have been good enough to write to me correcting or amplifying statements made in the first edition of this essay. My sincere thanks.

Mr Fred Hale, of the Nelson Inn, Merryvale, Worcester, comments on Aristotle (p. 44):

'You are not right. Aristotle to the public-house mind means: Aristotle=up the bottle=bottle and glass=up the x (Mr Wilde is a y . . .). There are other examples of rhyming slang in connection with words of abuse. E.g.: "Gehout you berk." Berk=Berkeley=Berkeley Hunt=z. By the way what is a *muck-horn*? "You are a bloody muck-horn." Muck-horn beats me.'

I do not know. Perhaps it is a cross between a wag-horn, or cuckold, and a muck-worm, or miser. It is a good word, anyhow.

Mr John Crow, of Worcester College, Oxford, complains that no mention is made of the splendidly scornful word 'git'. E.g.: '*You whore's git.*' He suggests that this word is an ancient one. 'Git is simply that which is gotten', he writes. I believe that he is wrong, and that it is *illegitimate child* reduced to a monosyllable.

Mr F. Jordan of Australia writes that the Australian poem is pre-War, having been quoted in the Sydney Law School in 1905.

Vice-Admiral John D. Kelly of the Mediterranean Fleet is more helpful still.

He writes that the poem appeared in the *Sydney Bulletin* in 1899, and that the author was one W. T. Goodie. He has been good enough to send me the original version:

'———'

(The Great Australian Adjective)
The sunburnt —— stockman stood,
And, in a dismal —— mood,
    Apostrophised his —— duddy;
'The —— nag's no —— good,
He couldn't earn his —— food—
    A regular —— brumby, (i.e. wild horse)
                            ——'!
He jumped across the —— horse
And cantered off, of —— course!
    The roads were bad and —— muddy;
Said he: 'Well, spare me —— days

THE FUTURE OF SWEARING

The —— Government's —— ways
  Are screamin' —— funny,
                                  ——!'

He rode up hill, down —— dale,
The wind it blew a —— gale.
  The creek was high and —— floody.
Said he: 'The —— horse must swim
The same for —— me and him,
  Is something —— sickenin',
                                  ——!'

He plunged into the —— creek,
The —— horse was —— weak,
  The stockman's face a —— study!
And though the —— horse was drowned
The —— rider reached the ground
  Ejaculating: '——?'
                           '——!'

Admiral Kelly comments on my footnote to page 12: *Brother-in-law* is a common expletive in Urdu, Arabic, and Swahili. I have always understood it to imply: 'I have been familiar with your sister, ergo, you are my brother-in-law.'

Mr Christopher Millard makes three valuable notes:

Page 10. Your account of the libellous card left

at Wilde's club is not quite accurate. Queensberry wrote on his own visiting card 'Oscar Wilde posing as a somdomite'—the words 'posing as' were inserted on legal advice and 'somdomite' was the marquess's quaint spelling. Queensberry handed the card to the porter of the Albemarle Club, who put it into an envelope and handed it to Wilde on his next visit to the club. So there was only technical 'publication'; but if Wilde had not taken action when he did, Queensberry would have gone on until he compelled Wilde to do something to protect himself.

Page 52. *The Times Literary Supplement,* of February 24, 1905, in reviewing Wilde's *De Profundis*: 'Not so, we find ourselves saying, are souls laid bare.'

Page 54. The Catholic doctrine of the Immaculate Conception refers to the B.V.M. and not to Christ. The doctrine is that the B.V.M. was not only born without original sin (as is held also of John the Baptist) but was conceived without the taint of original sin. The conception of Christ being held to be super-natural, there would be no question of Christ being conceived in sin or not.